RAGTIME C[

41 GREAT RAGTIME PIANO SOLOS
BY 20 FAMOUS COMPOSERS

INCLUDING SCOTT JOPLIN, IRVING BERLIN, EUBIE BLAKE, CLAUDE DEBUSSY AND ERIK SATIE

SELECTED AND EDITED BY MAURICE HINSON

AN ALFRED MASTERWORK EDITION

Cover art: The Bowery at Night, *1895*
by W. Louis Sonntag Jr. (1822–1900)
© Museum of the City of New York/Corbis

Contents

This volume is dedicated to Ingrid Clarfield with
admiration and appreciation.

Maurice Hinson

Foreword:
Ragtime Classics

Ragtime was extremely popular as an American musical form from its beginnings in the 1890s through its peak in 1915. With its lighthearted gaiety, ragtime encouraged people to forget about problems and simply have fun. Its infectious, syncopated beat make it sound fresh, and its appeal is just as strong today as when it first appeared.

This collection contains some of the greatest rags ever composed. The selections range from Mark Janza's *The Lion Tamer Rag*, with its surprising harmonies and syncopations, through the "classic" rag composer Scott Joplin, to the French composers Claude Debussy and Erik Satie, two of the greatest classical composers to use ragtime. A number of great rags by lesser-known composers are also included.

About This Edition

This collection is organized alphabetically by composer and title. Most of the repertoire is for the upper intermediate to the moderately advanced pianist. It can be used (1) for sheer enjoyment, (2) as a sight-reading supplement for advanced students, and (3) for receptions and other social events.

Performing the Music

A piano rag is a keyboard dance intended to inspire and accompany expressive physical motion. Most ragtime composers scored their rags carefully to be played as written. Scott Joplin said in his *School of Ragtime:* "The 'Joplin ragtime' is destroyed by careless or imperfect rendering, and very often good players lose the effect entirely by playing too fast. They [his rags] are harmonized with the supposition that each note will be played as it is written, as it takes this and also the proper time divisions to complete the sense intended." But small variations and embellishments may be added to a properly played rag, since Joplin and other ragtime composers did this in their own performances.

Much of the unique "feel" of these pieces results in using tempos that are neither hurried nor plodding. In 1905 Joplin began adding the following at the beginning of his rags: "Notice! Don't play this piece fast. It is never right to play 'ragtime' fast. Author." Other rag composers added similar directions.

Concerning the performance of a rag, Eubie Blake, the great ragtime composer and pianist suggests: "First learn it as written and then play it *your* way." The ragtime pianist's touch should be somewhat percussive and the damper pedal not often used. The player should aim for the good phrasing characteristic of all fine keyboard performances.

While some of these rags have instant appeal, others require a few more exposures before they too become favorites. Rags reward the persistent and attentive pianist with continual delightful surprises, as the selections in RAGTIME CLASSICS so ably demonstrate.

Editing

Great care has been given to the layout and engraving of this music. All fingerings and pedal indications are editorial unless stated otherwise. Dynamics, unless placed in parentheses, are the composer's original indications. Some rags use the dynamic indications *f*–*p* and/or *p*–*f*: *f*–*p* means that the section is to be played forte the first time and piano the second; *p*–*f* indicates the reverse. Suggested metronome markings have been added by the editor.

Dusty Rag

(1908)

May Frances Aufderheide
(1888–1972)

Alexander's Ragtime Band

(1911)

Irving Berlin
(1888–1989)

The Chevy Chase

(1914)

James Hubert (Eubie) Blake
(1883–1983)

ⓐ All pedal indications are Blake's.

Twelfth Street Rag

(1914)

Euday Louis Bowman
(1887–1949)

Lively ($\musHalfNote$ = ca. 76)

ⓐ Cue-sized notes are optional.

19

Golliwogg's Cakewalk

from *Children's Corner*

(1908)

Claude Achille Debussy
(1862–1918)

(a) All pedal indications are editorial.

(A little slower)
Un peu moins vite

ⓑ The fingerings in italics are Debussy's.

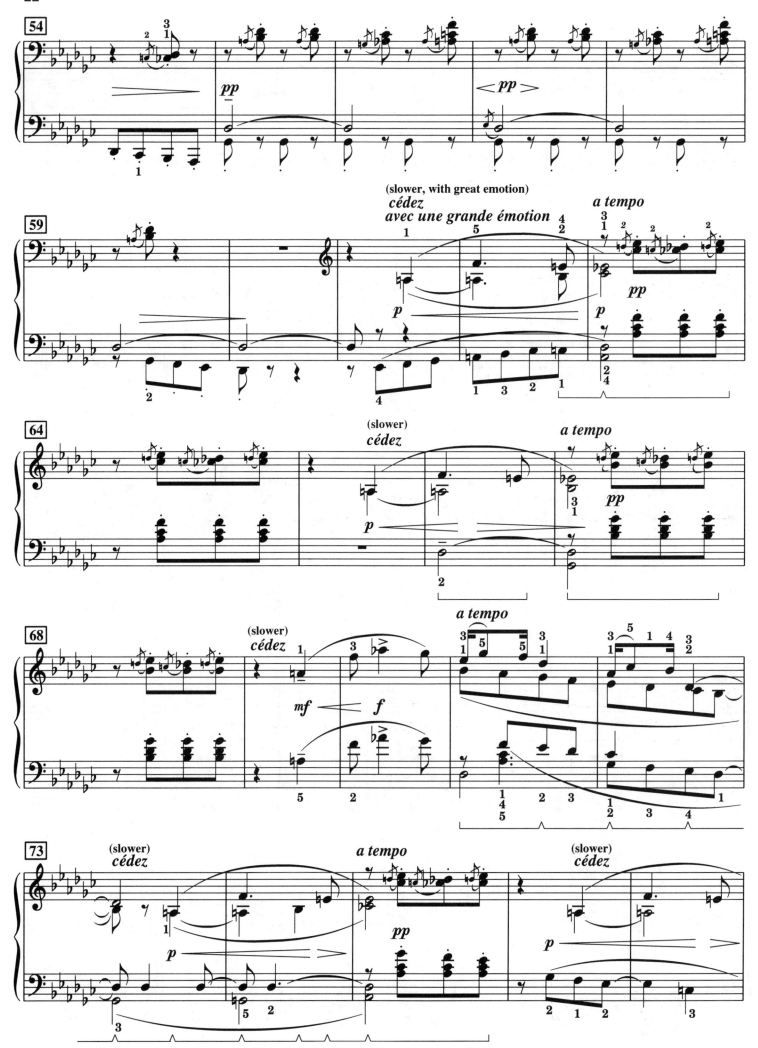

Le petit Nègre

Cakewalk

(1909)

Claude Achille Debussy
(1862–1918)

ⓐ All pedal indications are editorial.

The Memphis Blues

(1912)

William Christopher (W. C.) Handy
(1873–1958)

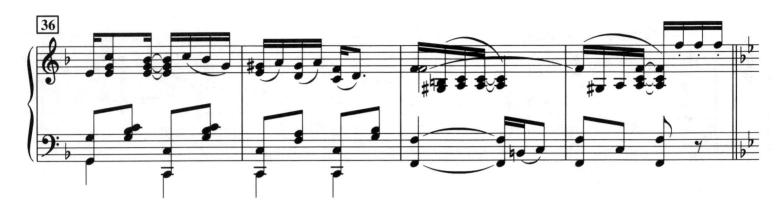

St. Louis Blues
(1914)

William Christopher (W. C.) Handy
(1873–1958)

ⓐ All pedal indications are Handy's.

Smoky Mokes

Cakewalk and Two Step

(1899)

Abraham (Abe) Holzmann
(1874–1939)

ⓐ Cue-sized notes are optional.

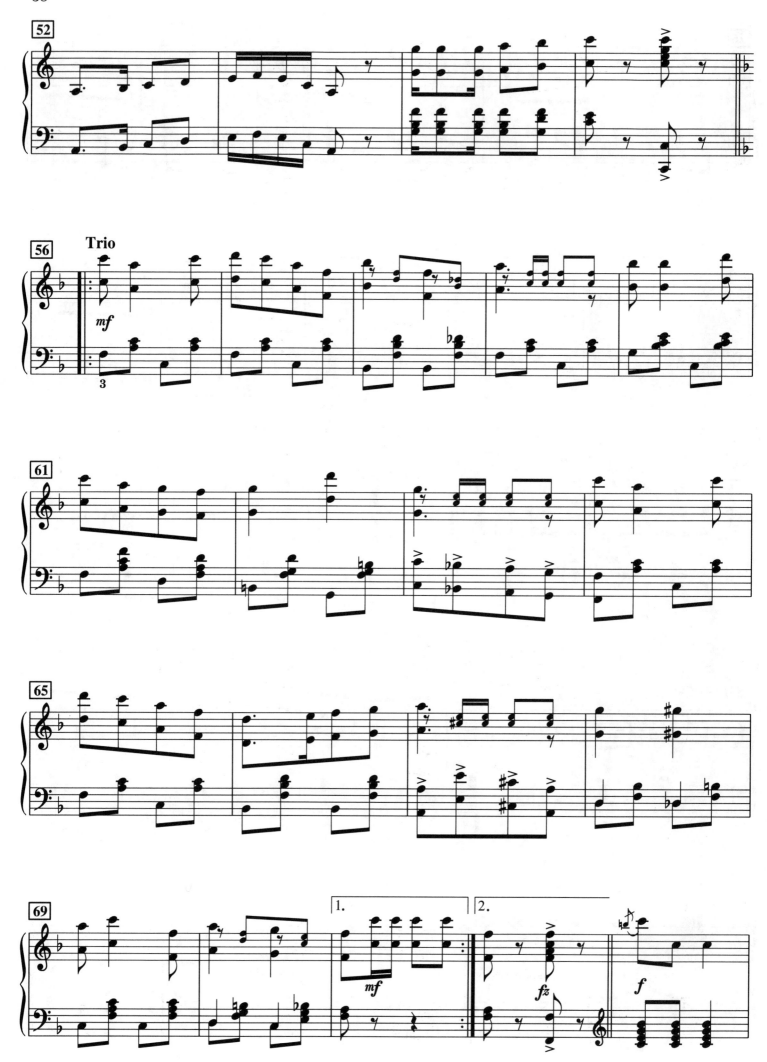

The Lion Tamer Rag

A Syncopated Fantasia

(1913)

Mark Janza
(dates unknown)

(a) The fingerings in italics are Janza's.

(b) Cue-sized notes are optional.

42

Dill Pickles Rag

A Ragtime Two Step

(1906)

Charles Leslie Johnson
(1876–1950)

48

Bethena

A Concert Waltz

(1905)

Scott Joplin
(1868–1917)

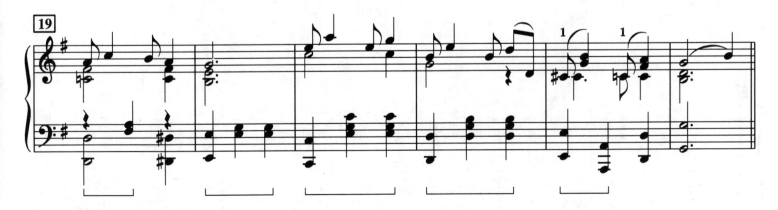

ⓐ All pedal indications are Joplin's.

A Breeze from Alabama

March and Two Step

(1902)

Scott Joplin
(1868–1917)

The Cascades

A Rag

(1904)

Scott Joplin
(1868–1917)

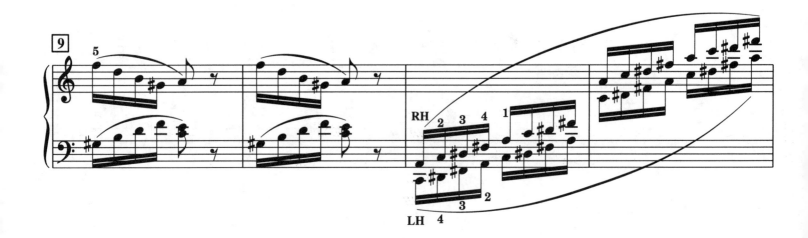

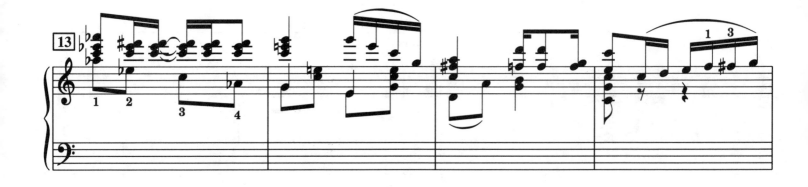

61

(a) All pedal indications are Joplin's, but the editor recommends using less pedal than Joplin suggests.

Cleopha

March and Two Step

(1902)

Scott Joplin
(1868–1917)

The Chrysanthemum

An African-American Intermezzo

(1904)

Slow march tempo (♩ = ca. 66)

Scott Joplin
(1868–1917)

ⓐ All pedal indications are Joplin's.

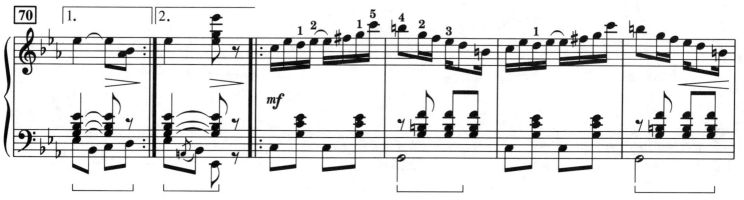

The Easy Winners

A Ragtime Two Step

(1901)

Scott Joplin
(1868–1917)

Not fast (♩ = ca. 72)

ⓐ *mf*

f – p

f – p

ⓐ All dynamics are editorial.

ⓑ The fingerings in italics are Joplin's.

Elite Syncopations

(1902)

Scott Joplin
(1868–1917)

The Entertainer

A Ragtime Two Step

(1902)

Scott Joplin
(1868–1917)

Heliotrope Bouquet

A Slow Drag Two Step

(1907)

Scott Joplin (1868–1917)
and Louis Chauvin (1881–1908)

Maple Leaf Rag

(1899)

Scott Joplin
(1868–1917)

Tempo di marcia (♩ = ca. 88)

ⓐ All cue-sized notes in this piece are the embellishments Joplin played on repeats in his piano roll of this rag.

91

ⓑ Play cue-sized notes on repeat only.

Original Rags

(1899)

Scott Joplin
(1868–1917)

94

Peacherine Rag
(1901)

Scott Joplin
(1868–1917)

ⓐ All dynamics are editorial.

The Ragtime Dance

A Stop-Time Two Step

(1906)

Scott Joplin
(1868–1917)

NOTICE: To get the desired effect of "Stop Time" the pianist will please **Stamp** the heel of one foot heavily upon the floor at the word "Stamp." Do not raise the toe from the floor while stamping.

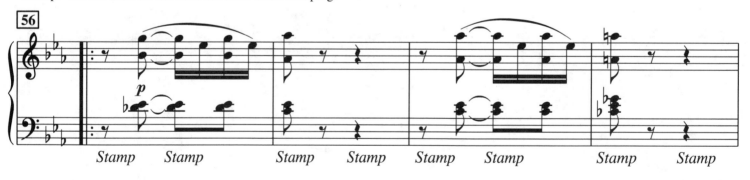

Stamp   *Stamp*   *Stamp*   *Stamp*   *Stamp*   *Stamp*   *Stamp*   *Stamp*

Stamp   *Stamp*   *Stamp*   *Stamp*   *Stamp*   *Stamp*   *Stamp*
                                                                                  Stamp

Solace
A Mexican Serenade
(1909)

Scott Joplin
(1868–1917)

Very slow march time (♩ = ca. 63)

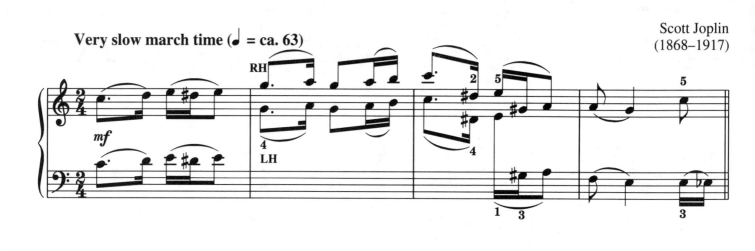

ⓐ Pedal indications in measures 22–36 are Joplin's.

The Strenuous Life

A Ragtime Two Step

(1902)

Scott Joplin
(1868–1917)

Sunflower Slow Drag

A Ragtime Two Step

(1901)

Scott Joplin (1868–1917)
and Scott Hayden (1882–1915)

Swipesy

Cakewalk

(1900)

Scott Joplin (1868–1917)
and Arthur Marshall (1881–1968)

119

Weeping Willow

A Ragtime Two Step

(1903)

Scott Joplin
(1868–1917)

Ragtime Nightingale

(1915)

Joseph Francis Lamb
(1887–1960)

Slow march tempo ($\quarternote$ = ca. 66)

Sensation

A Rag

(1908)

Joseph Francis Lamb
(1887–1960)

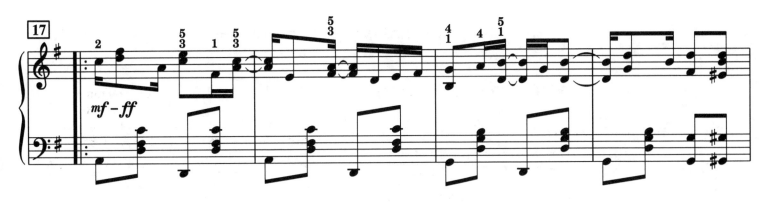

Red Pepper Rag

(1910)

Thomas Henry Lodge
(1884 –1933)

ⓐ Composer's tempo indication.

This march was not intended to be a part of the religious exercises "at a Georgia campmeeting"—but when the young folks got together they felt as if they needed some amusement. A cakewalk was suggested and held in a quiet place nearby—hence this music.

At a Georgia Campmeeting

March

(1897)

Kerry Mills
(1869–1948)

(a) Cue-sized notes are optional.

Hoosier Rag

March Two Step
(1907)

Julia Lee Niebergall
(1886–1968)

ⓐ Cue-sized notes are optional.

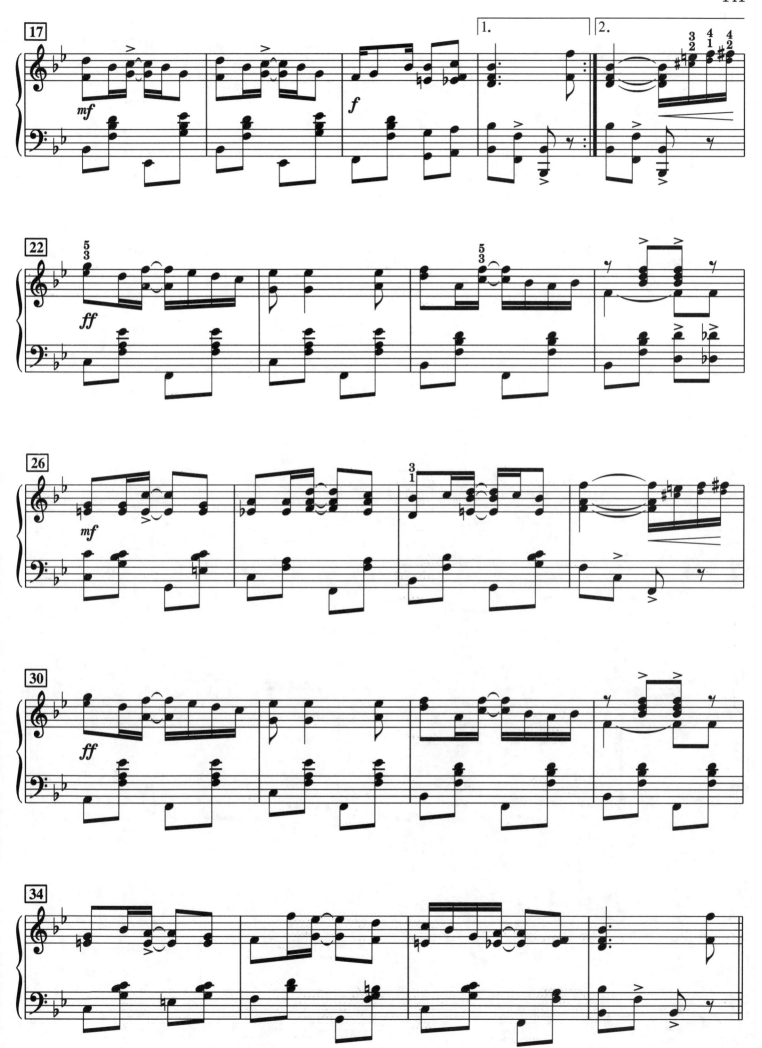

Pork and Beans

One Step–Two Step or Turkey Trot

(1913)

Charles Luckeyth (Lucky) Roberts
(1887–1968)

(Moderato ♩ = ca. 76)

ⓐ Cue-sized notes are optional.

Le Piccadilly

Marche

(1904)

Erik Satie
(1866–1925)

(a) All pedal indications are editorial.

Grace and Beauty

A Classy Rag

(1909)

James Sylvester Scott
(1885–1938)

Do not play this piece fast. (a)

(Moderato ♩ = ca. 72)

(a) Composer's tempo indication.

(b) The fingerings in italics are Scott's.

Pickles and Peppers

(1906)

Adaline Shepherd
(1883–1950)

(a) Play both hands one octave higher than notated in measures 63–78. Play as written beginning at measure 79.

Harlem Rag

(1897) ⓐ

Thomas M. J. Turpin
(1873–1922)

(Play a little slow ♩ = ca. 76)

ⓐ Copyright date—date of composition unknown.

The St. Louis Rag

(1903)

Thomas M. J. Turpin
(1873–1922)

Allegretto (♩ = ca. 76)

Peaches and Cream

A Delectable Rag

(1905)

Percy Wenrich
(1887–1952)

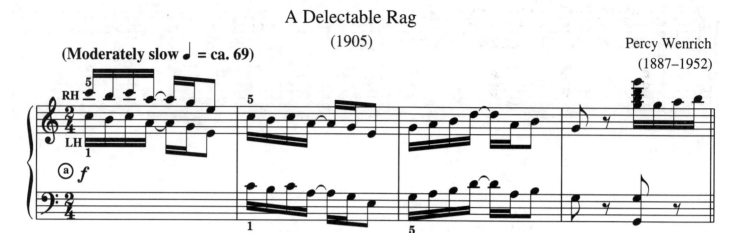

ⓐ All dynamics are editorial.

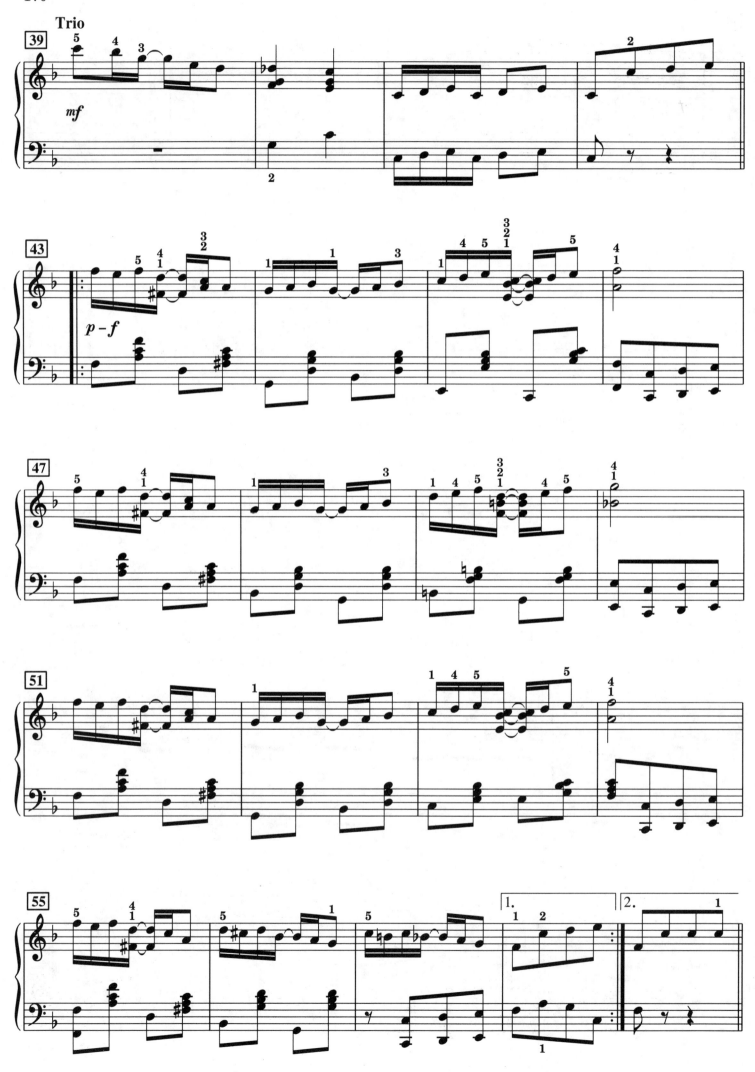